Catch of the day

How to buy, store and cook
North Atlantic seafood

Paul McCormick

Acknowledgements

The publisher wishes to express his appreciation for the financial support of the Nova Scotia Department of Tourism and Culture.

Richard Rogers, Publisher

1st printing May 1990
2nd printing February 1996

Edited by Grayce Rogers
Layout and design by Paul McCormick
Typesetting, printing and binding by McCurdy Printing (1995) Limited, Halifax, Nova Scotia, Canada

Published by

Four East Publications
P.O. Box 29
Tantallon, Nova Scotia   B0J 3J0

ISBN 0-920427-24-3

The *Scotia Bouillabaisse* on our cover is courtesy of the Nova Scotia Department of Fisheries.

For Paige and Kelsey

Acknowledgements

I'd like to thank Pat Crowdis, Monique Michalik, Sue Ann McCleave, Linda McCormick and Elaine Piper for contributing recipes or research material for this book. I should also thank Richard Gilbert for his assistance with the last rewrite. A special acknowledgement goes to Brian Giroux, who has been a fisherman, fisheries observer, organizer and pretty mean seafood cook for the past decade and a half. He graciously reviewed this manuscript for accuracy and supplied much of the background so necessary to a land dweller dealing with marine life.

Contents

Fish: An old foodsource for a new age

It was the abundance of codfish off the east coast of North America which first brought the Portuguese and Bretons to our shores in the 15th century. And while it was furs that attracted the English and French, it was the fish that held their interest.

Southwestern Nova Scotia, home of the richest inshore fishery on the east coast, was first settled by fishermen from New England some twenty years before the arrival of the United Empire Loyalists in the 1780s.

While annual quotas vary, some one million tons of fish are caught within the 200 mile limit off the northeast coast of North America each and every year. Outside the 200 mile limit, some 200 foreign vessels are estimated to be taking upwards of 7,000 tons a day. That's a lot of fish!

While the basis for government regulations is changing from boat length to volume, the industry is best summed up by the latter. When we talk about fishing, we are really talking about three quite separate pursuits: the inshore fishery, made up of boats under 45 feet in length; the midshore fishery, with vessels ranging from 45 to 65 feet; and the offshore fleet of larger ships which may process some or all of their catch while at sea.

The inshore fishery is that arm of the industry which supplies the majority of fresh market fish to consumers. Made up of smaller boats employing one to four people, inshore fishermen generally sail at dawn and return to port the same evening, icing their catch and selling it fresh to local wholesalers and small community packing plants, or trucking it to the New Bedford and Boston markets. The inshore fishery employs most of those we know as fishermen.

The midshore fleet is composed of slightly larger boats

which generally fish farther offshore on the "banks" which stretch from Labrador south to Cape Hatteras. While some of their catch may be sold fresh, most is processed as frozen fish. A midshore fishing trip may last from two days to a week.

The offshore fleet, sailing from major ports and large processing plants, provides most of our institutional fish. Trips may last as long as one month. A few employ onboard freezing facilities, and some are actually processing plants disguised as ships. Commercial fishsticks, institutional packs of single-portion pieces and specialty items for restaurant chains are all supplied by the offshore fleet.

The fresh fish being sold at your local supermarket or fish market has most likely been caught fairly recently by an inshore boat.

Seafood: An environmental yardstick

Even the most diehard fish fanatic may wonder about the safety of this foodsource given the increasing alarm over the sorry condition of our marine environment. But the fact is, fish are extremely sensitive to environmental damage. It is this sensitivity which makes them an ideal instrument to measure the condition of local ecosystems.

Fish, unlike the mammals which predominantly make up the human diet, are comparatively simple, cold-blooded organisms. They act as an initial environmental indicator; if the temperature of the water is not right, fish will simply not inhabit it. The same applies in the case of chemical or industrial pollution, which will often cause obvious malformations in individual fish, such as organs misplaced on the outside instead of inside their bodies, extra appendages and other horrors of mutation. Fish are very good indicators of the condition of our oceans.

The original free-range foodsource

The willingness of the consumer to pay extra for free-range meat, i.e. animals which have been allowed to graze freely rather than being penned and force-fed, has been amply demonstrated in recent years. Fish, with the exception of a few varieties now raised in aquaculture operations, range as far afield as temperature and food necessitate. And like other free-range animals, fish are a healthier source of food for humans than the force-fed products of agribusiness.

Fish has fewer calories than meat. A single serving supplies one-third to one-half the daily protein requirement as well as B vitamins, thiamin, niacin and riboflavin. A diet of fish is also rich in copper, iron, calcium and phosphorus.

Fish is low in fat and high in fatty acids such as omega-3. These fatty acids have actually been demonstrated to reduce cholesterol in the bloodstream.

Many of the recipes in this book call for the use of butter. Butter is a personal preference in the cooking of fish; its distinctive flavour complements the mild taste of seafood. In most instances a small amount of butter is called for in combination with vegetable oil. Combining butter with oil reduces the cholesterol content of the finished dish and prevents the butter from browning when brought to a high temperature. If you prefer, you may use only vegetable oil, without greatly affecting the flavour of the finished dish.

Identifying dinner

Fish is sold in a wide variety of forms ranging from whole fish to trimmed fillets. The following pages should assist you in understanding the vocabulary of shopping for seafood.

Whole fish is sold in the same state as when caught. *Gutted* fish is whole fish which has been slit along the abdomen and the digestive tract and organs removed. The head may or may not be still attached. Gutted fish is also known as *dressed* fish.

The removal of skin, head, tail, bones and fins from gutted fish yields *fillets*. Gutted fish which has been sliced crosswise creates *steaks*. *Roasts* are cut from larger species of fish in much the same size range as that of regular meat.

Fish

Atlantic Salmon

A member of the same family as trout and arctic char, the Atlantic salmon has silvery scales with some black spotting. They average in weight from three to 20 pounds and are caught from southwest Greenland to as far south as Maine.

Small salmon are usually sold whole, dressed with head, tail and skin intact. Larger fish are sold as steaks, roasts and only occasionally, fillets.

Trout

A close relative of the Atlantic salmon, most trout available in markets is from commercial aquaculture operations. Trout are sold whole or dressed and range from one-half to two pounds in weight.

Smelts

The capelin and rainbow smelt, relatives of the trout, range in size from nine to 13 inches and are found feeding near the surface in schools from Greenland to New Jersey. Smelts are netted or fished through holes in the ice on inland bays during the winter months.

Smelts are sold fresh or frozen in packages of several whole fish.

Flounder and Sole

What we see in our fish markets labelled as "sole" is most often greysole (witch flounder), winter flounder, summer flounder (fluke), American plaice or yellowtail.

Flounders range in length from one to 25 inches, are very flat with the eyes both on the top side, brownish with spots ranging from black to yellow. Flounder is caught from Greenland south to the mid-Atlantic states.

Flounder and sole are most often sold as fresh or frozen fillets.

Halibut

Halibut, a flat fish and the largest of Atlantic flounders, is generally grey and somewhat mottled with a white underside.

While nine-foot halibut were once common, most now range in size from two to seven feet and are found throughout the northeastern Atlantic.

Small halibut (3-5 lbs.) are available whole and dressed for baking. Larger fish are sold as roasts, steaks and, occasionally, fillets.

Turbot

Also know as "Greenland halibut", turbot is found around

Baffin Island, Greenland and throughout the northeastern Atlantic.

Turbot is flat - like other flounders - and uniform grey or brown. They range up to three feet in length, and are generally sold as fresh fillets.

Ocean Perch

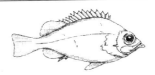

Ocean perch is the marketing name for golden, deepwater and Acadian redfish. Whole fish are golden to red in colour and have a marked bony protuberance on the chin.

They range in length from just under one foot to 20 inches. While their habitat stretches from Greenland to New Jersey, most are caught in the Gulf of St. Lawrence, on the Scotia Shelf and in the Gulf of Maine.

Once considered "trash fish", ocean perch is now commonly sold as fresh or frozen fillets.

Mackerel

In the late spring and early summer when mackerel are 'running', the waters off bridges and causeways along the coast appears to boil with hundreds of dark silver-blue bodies. A closer examination will reveal 20 to 30 wavy black bars across the backs and small finlets behind the main fins.

Mackerel range in size up to two pounds and are sold as whole dressed and undressed fish or filleted and smoked.

Cod

The Atlantic cod is one of the world's most important commercial fishes. With a variable body colour, brownish spots and whitish belly, the codfish is most readily distinguished by its short lower jaw.

Found throughout the northeastern Atlantic as far south as Cape Hatteras, cod range in weight from two to ten pounds and are most often sold as fresh or frozen fillets. Cod is also popular as dried salted scraps, smoked, and very thin dried fillets.

Haddock

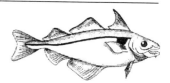

Haddock looks much like its less beautiful cousin the cod, except instead of being reddish brown it is a dark purple-grey on its back, fading through silver sides to a white belly.

Size and habitat are similar to the cod. Haddock is sold as fresh or frozen fillets and, occasionally as whole, dressed fish. It is also smoked as fillets, or sides with skin and fins intact and sold as "finnan haddie".

Pollock

You may find pollock sold as "Boston bluefish." It is

similar in appearance to haddock, except with a protruding lower jaw.

Habitat and size are similar to the closely related cod and haddock.

Pollock is available as fresh or frozen fillets or as salted, dried scraps.

Tuna

The bluefin tuna reputedly reaches sizes of up to 14 feet and weights of 1500 pounds, although most are nearer half that size. Bluefin tuna is caught in the Gulf of St. Lawrence and off northeastern North America.

When available as fresh fish, tuna is usually sold as steaks or roasts. Most canned tuna are species other than bluefin and are caught from the Gulf of Mexico south to Argentina

---

Swordfish

The swordfish is perhaps the most easily recognizable Atlantic fish. These large fish inhabit the waters from Nova Scotia south to Brazil. Due to a combination of size, lifespan and range, swordfish has been unavailable for periods of time because of a tendency for its meat to contain measureable levels of mercury.

Swordfish are dark on top and pale below with no spots or other markings. Their most prominent feature is a sword-like upper jaw which may reach four feet in length. Average size is 200 to 400 pounds.

Swordfish is usually sold as steaks of a reddish-brown colour.

Herring

Herring are silver-blue fish of up to one foot in length found feeding in schools near the surface from northern Labrador south to North Carolina.

Herring are sold as fresh, whole, dressed fish, smoked, dried, salted, pickled and canned as sardines. They are also extensively used as bait by the commercial fishery and lobster industry.

Monkfish (Lotte)

The monkfish, or more properly, goosefish, is from one to three feet in length and easily recognizable because of its disproportionately large head. They range from Quebec to northern Florida, offshore in the deeper waters of the continental shelf.

Monkfish is usually sold as fresh or frozen tails.

Shellfish

Lobster

The lobster is a marine crustacean inhabiting the north Atlantic from coastal Newfoundland south to New Jersey. Lobsters are ten-legged, the two front legs taking the form of enlarged claws. Lobsters range in size from a few inches to several feet in length, although the "market lobster" generally weighs from one to three pounds. Live lobsters are generally a greenish black in their natural environment.

Market lobsters are fished throughout the coastal regions of the northeastern Atlantic by inshore and, in a few areas, the midshore fleets. There is also a small offshore industry bringing in catches consisting of larger lobsters ranging in weight from three to twenty-five pounds.

The inshore fishery, which supplies the majority of market lobsters, fishes at different times of the year depending on designated zones. In the Gulf of St. Lawrence and eastern shore of Nova Scotia, the season lasts from mid-spring to mid-fall. On the south shore of Nova Scotia and the Bay of Fundy, it is a winter fishery with the highest catch landings in early December and May. In New England, the fishery operates year-round, with strict size limitations imposed on catches.

Because lobster fishing is potentially a high-income fishery (with winter prices reaching as high as six dollars a pound) and involves a finite resource, the Canadian industry has limited entry. Currently, the only way for a new Canadian fisherman to begin catching lobsters is to actually purchase an existing boat and license. In the United States, the industry is much more open, to the point where individuals may trap lobsters in small numbers privately for their personal consumption.

Throughout the region lobsters are caught in traps which are set with floating buoys to mark their locations. These traps are checked regularly, and legal-sized lobsters removed. The traditional lobster trap is constructed of wood with one or two conically netted entrances which allow the lobster to crawl in and feed on the bait but make it impossible for it to get out again.

Live fresh lobster is available year-round. Look for active lobsters with moving legs. When the lobster is picked up, the tail should curl under its body. Lobsters should cook to a bright red colour. Cooked (boiled) lobster is sold either fresh or frozen. Pre-cooked, shelled and flash-frozen lobster meat is also marketed in tins and plastic tubs.

Crab

The snow crab is the most important north Atlantic food crab. Also known as the spider or queen crab, it is fished in the Gulf of St. Lawrence from June to October. The average size is three pounds, although meat weight is only about one-third of this. Snow crab is available frozen or canned.

The blue crab is fished from Cape Cod south to the Gulf of Mexico. This catch accounts for half of the crab consumed by North Americans. Also, watch for Pacific species at the frozen fish counter, such as Dungeness and Alaska king crab.

Clams

Soft-shell or steamer clams are dug in the tidal flats surrounding the Bay of Fundy. They range in size from one to four inches.

When purchased live and fresh, shells should be tightly closed and unbroken. If the shells twist easily when force is applied; or can be pried open, then the animal inside is no longer alive. When shelled, the liquor should be clear and sweet smelling and the meat firm and plump. Clams are also available cooked and canned, breaded and frozen.

Mussels

The blue mussel is widely distributed along the coast of the northeastern Atlantic, held in dense clusters by means of a tough byssal thread (or beard) along the rocks and pilings in intertidal zones.

This bluish-black bivalve is available in two forms: wild and cultured. Cultured mussels are grown in aquaculture operations throughout Canada's Maritime Provinces and northern New England. Canadian mussel farmers grow mussels on lines suspended from ropes strung between buoys. Most American operations employ bottom culture in which "spat" is seeded in areas where the farmer wishes beds to form. Cultured mussels, in particular those grown using line culture, are free from the grit sometimes found in wild or bottom culture, and also carry almost twice as much meat in their shells.

Mussels are purchased fresh, in the shell. Fresh mussels should be iced well. Shells should be tightly closed and unbroken. If the shells twist easily when force is applied, or can be pried open, then the animal inside is no longer alive. When shelled, the liquor should be clear and sweet smelling and the meat firm and plump. Shells should open when steamed.

Oysters

The origin of an oyster is often evident from its name; Bras d'Or, Malpeque, Cape Cod and Chesapeake suggest the wide range these molluscs inhabit. Oysters grow naturally in warm intertidal zones, but are most often raised in aquaculture operations using bottom culture. "Spat" is seeded in areas where the farmer wishes beds to form.

Oysters are available fresh, in the shell and should be sold well iced. Shells should be tightly closed and unbroken. If the shells twist easily when force is applied, then the animal inside is no longer alive. When shelled, the liquor should be clear and sweet smelling and the meat firm and plump.

Shrimp

Shrimp, or prawns, are the most popular shellfish on the North American market. They are fished throughout the northeastern Atlantic.

Shrimp are sold by the count, i.e. the number of animals to the pound. This may range from as low as 8-10 for jumbo shrimp to as high as 180 for salad shrimp. Shrimp are available fresh, on ice and frozen. While there is a great variance in the colour of raw shrimp, all shrimp should cook to a nice pinkish colour. Salad shrimp may also be purchased frozen in tubs and canned.

Scallops

Sea scallops are bivalves found mainly on the banks off the shore of Nova Scotia and in the Gulf of Maine. It is the muscle which is eaten by North Americans, although the roe is considered a delicacy in Japan and Europe. Sea scallops are graded by the size of the muscle, or number of "meats" per pound. This muscle may be as large as three inches across.

The bay scallop's muscle is under one inch in size. Some limited bay scallop fishery exists and the species is also being tried in aquaculture.

Scallops are sold fresh or frozen. Fresh scallops should be a white or pinkish white colour and smell sweet when purchased.

Aquaculture

Just as the human race evolved from gatherers to growers of food on land several millenia ago, the fishing industry in the last two decades has been making a similar transformation, at least in the production of several species.

Perhaps the oldest form of the aquaculture industry in North America is the production of oysters using bottom culture. Molluscs release "spat" or microscopic larvae which float with the tide in sheltered, coastal regions during the month of July. This spat can be harvested using fine mesh bags towed behind boats, and used as seed for shellfish aquaculture such as mussel and oyster beds.

A great advance in aquaculture has come with string culture. A long line is strung between two buoys. Shorter "strings" are hung vertically, evenly spaced along this line, with each string supported by a floating buoy. Shellfish at the end of its larval stage naturally attaches to ropes, rocks, pilings or whatever solid surface happens to be available. Spat which has been gathered is placed in mesh stockings and secured to the ends of these strings, where it is allowed to develop for up to eighteen months. The strings can be weighted to float below the ice in winter. The shellfish are safe from starfish, seagulls and other predators, and the mature animals are free from grit, pearls and impurities.

Oysters and mussels are commonly raised in aquaculture operations, and other projects involving species such as clams and scallops are being developed.

The second aspect of aquaculture is fish farming. Quite common in Scandinavia, fish farming techniques in North America have, until recently, been used mainly to raise "fingerlings" of trout and salmon for release in rivers and streams as sport fish. The declining natural stocks of Atlantic salmon and the resulting escalating price has made farming of this and other species an economically viable proposition.

Salmon and trout are penned in inland bays and coves, fed a controlled diet and harvested when they reach a marketable size. Experimentation with the closely related arctic char is also taking place, and new species which combine the better traits of salmon and char may well soon be introduced commercially.

Aquaculture has several advantages over the traditional fishing industry. First, the controls are more manageable. Environmental quality can be readily and regularly monitored. The health of the marine animal being raised is easily assessed, as is the safety of the harvested product. Also, the marketer can easily target production levels and species types to meet market demand and the closely connected factor of market price. Farmers are able to provide a regular, uninterrupted supply.

Secondly, the product is more attractive. Fish and molluscs raised in aquaculture operations can be harvested at uniform market sizes and quality. Shellfish is cleaner and free of grit. All species yield higher meat content when raised in a controlled environment. The product is fresher and will keep longer.

Buying fish

Fresh

When buying fish, your main consideration should be the freshness.

Fresh fish should be sold well iced. The flesh should never feel slimy. If buying whole fish, the eyes must be clear, bright and slightly bulging. Fillets should be translucent and predominantly white in colour, although some species may have a golden or pinkish tinge. Cut edges should not be dry.

Fresh fish should never have a strong "fishy" odour, but rather a light, only slight, scent of the ocean.

Frozen

Frozen fillets can be as high quality as fresh, if they have been iced when caught and processed properly while still fresh. Frozen fillets should be encased in a thin shell of ice under the plastic wrapper. They should not have any ice crystals or dry, white spots, edges or corners suggesting "freezer burn", or discolouration of any kind.

To thaw frozen fish, rinse to remove the glaze, and then allow to thaw slowly while covered in the refrigerator. The fish should be cooked as soon as thawing is completed.

Some basic rules for cooking fish

➤ Fish, unlike meat, has no connective tissue and does not require slow cooking.

➤ Fish is cooked when the interior temperature of its thickest flesh reaches 140°F.

➤ Fish is overcooked when its temperature reaches 150°F.

➤ Fish is fully cooked when the flesh turns from a translucent to opaque white and flakes easily.

➤ Fish cooked in the microwave should be allowed to stand covered for at least five minutes after baking to ensure that it is cooked evenly throughout.

➤ As with cake baking, a clean stick or straw inserted into cooked fish will come away clean and free of flesh. Likewise, cooked fish will spring back when prodded with a finger.

➤ Use the "ten minute rule" when cooking fish. Fish may be timed by cooking ten minutes for each inch of thickness. This includes whole fish which have been stuffed.

Stovetop Recipes

Pan Fried Haddock Fillets

4 haddock fillets
2 tablespoons vegetable oil
2 teaspoons butter
salt
pepper
lemon juice

Rinse fillets under cool running water. Gently dry with clean towel.

Warm large skillet over medium/high heat, then add oil and butter. Heat oil until hot enough to sear fish, but not smoking. Cook fillets, turning twice, 3 to 4 minutes until flesh flakes and loses its translucence. Sprinkle with lemon, salt and pepper and serve immediately.

Serves 4.

Substitutions: Cod, Halibut, Pollock, Sole.

A sprinkle of chopped fresh tarragon accents a fillet's delicate flavour.

Scallops sautéed in butter

1 lb. scallops
2 tablespoons oil
1 tablespoon butter
1 tablespoon lemon juice
2 tablespoons dry sherry
pepper

Rinse scallops under cool running water and pat dry.
Heat skillet over medium heat. Add oil and butter. Add
scallops, cook until outside edges of scallops turn white; about
two minutes. Flip scallops, sprinkle with pepper, lemon juice
and sherry. Cover and simmer for two minutes. Increase heat,
uncover and shake to prevent scorching until liquid has evapo-
rated.
Serves 4.

*A sprinkle of chopped fresh tarragon, basil, fennel or mint will
enhance the flavour of the scallops without masking their delicate
flavour.*

Wok Stir Fry

¼ lb. scallops
½ lb. salmon, cut in 1-inch cubes
¼ lb. shrimp
½ cup broccoli florets
½ cup diced carrots
1 green pepper, cut into strips
½ cup bean sprouts (optional)
¼ cup celery
1 small onion, cut in rings
3 tablespoons oil
2 tablespoons soy sauce
2 tablespoons pineapple juice

½ teaspoon ground ginger
dash hot sauce

Heat oil in wok over medium high heat. Add broccoli, celery, carrots, green pepper and sprouts in succession, and drag to sides as each is coated and partially cooked. Place scallops, shrimp, salmon in centre of wok and cook for two to three minutes, turning until pieces lose translucence. Sprinkle with soy sauce, ginger, hot sauce and pineapple juice and stir and cook for two minutes or until liquid has been reduced.
Serves 6.

Swordfish, monkfish, clams, crabmeat or any firm-fleshed seafood may be substituted.

Fried Smelts

1 lb. cleaned smelts
1 egg, beaten
1 tablespoon lemon juice
½ cup flour
⅓ cup grated parmesan cheese
⅓ cup corn meal
1 teaspoon salt
¼ teaspoon pepper
fresh parsley
6-8 thin lemon slices

Combine egg and lemon juice. Combine flour, salt and pepper. In a third bowl combine cheese and cornmeal.

Dredge smelts in flour, dip in egg and roll in corn meal mixture. Pan fry, a few at a time in ¼-inch of oil over medium heat. Remove smelts to hot platter. Increase heat and singe lemon slices and parsley sprigs for garnish.
Serves 4.

Crab Cakes

8 oz. salad crabmeat
1 cup fine bread crumbs
3 tablespoons mayonnaise
1 tablespoon prepared mustard
2 tablespoons dried or ¼ cup fresh parsley
1 teaspoon salt
2-3 dashes hot sauce

Squeeze excess liquid from crabmeat. Combine ingredients and form into patties. Cook 8 to 10 minutes per side, or until golden and crisp.
Makes 8 crab cakes.

Halibut Fillets in Orange Sauce

1½-2 lbs. halibut fillets
3 tablespoons vegetable oil
½ cup butter, melted and cooled but still liquid
3 egg yolks
¼ cup orange juice, heated
1 tablespoon orange brandy or triple sec
1 teaspoon grated orange rind
½ teaspoon dry mustard
¼ teaspoon salt
fresh parsley for garnish

Heat oil in large skillet. Cook halibut over moderate heat, turning once, 10-12 minutes or until flesh is opaque and flakes with a fork. Carefully remove to a warm serving platter.

Place egg yolks in top of double boiler over, not in, boiling water. Add cooled butter and beat with a wire whisk until it begins to thicken, Add hot orange juice 1 tablespoon at a time, beating until thickened. After final tablespoon of orange juice has been added, beat in liqueur, rind, mustard and salt. Pour sauce over halibut, garnish with parsley and serve immediately. **Serves 4.**

Substitutions: Any mild-tasting fish such as sole or turbot.

Poached Fillets

4 fish fillets (1½-2 lbs.)
6 quarts water
2 medium onions, chopped
2 stalks celery, chopped
¼ cup butter
salt
pepper

Traditionally, fish is poached in parchment. With true parchment difficult to find, most cooks now use aluminum foil.

For each fillet, fold a large piece of foil, twice as long as its width, to make a square. Grease one side. Place fillet in centre of foil and dot with butter, onion and celery. Double-fold the edges to make a watertight pouch. Place in rapidly boiling water, reduce heat and simmer 10-12 minutes. Remove from foil and serve with onion and celery.
Serves 4.

Steamed Crab

6-8 live queen, snow or rock crab
6 quarts water
¼ cup salt
½ cup butter, melted
3-4 dashes hot sauce

Choose lively crabs 4-5 inches across the body.

Have salted water boiling furiously in large, deep kettle. Drop crabs head first, one at a time into water. Cover and cook 15-20 minutes, then quench in cold water.

Serve whole crabs with melted butter and hot sauce.
Serves 4.

Steamed Lobster

4 small to medium live lobsters (4-5 lbs. in total)
4 quarts water
¼ cup salt
½ cup butter
black pepper

Have salted water boiling furiously in large, deep kettle. Grasp lobsters, one at a time, from the back behind claws and drop head first into water. If claws are bound with elastics, remove them before cooking or lobster meat will have a slight rubberish taste. Hold lobster near pot with one hand and snip bands with scissors just before you introduce it to the kettle Cover and cook 20-22 minutes. Remove from hot water, quench with cold water and allow to drain. Crack hard edge of each claw with a heavy cleaver. Serve with drawn butter and freshly ground black pepper.
Serves 4.

Steamed Tuna

2-4 lbs. tuna (one "roast")
1 cup water
1 cup dry white wine
1 medium onion
1 bay leaf
2 springs fresh parsley
½ teaspoon salt

Combine water, wine, onion, bay leaf, parsley and salt in bottom of large, deep kettle. Cover and bring to a boil, reduce heat and simmer for 30 minutes.

Wipe tuna with damp cloth. Place in kettle with liquid, cover kettle and simmer 10-12 minutes for each inch of thickness, or until thermometer inserted to centre of fish reads 140° F. Remove from liquid and allow to cool. Refrigerate in covered container and substitute for canned tuna in any recipes.

Steamed Mussels

3 lbs. cultured mussels
½ cup dry white wine
or
½ cup water with 1 teaspoon salt

½ cup butter
8 shallots, chopped
1 clove garlic, finely chopped

A mussel, after refrigeration, should be closed. Discard any with open shells. Further inspect by trying to slide the top against the bottom of shell. If shell moves, there is more likely mud than mussel inside.

Scrub under running water, removing beards. Cook mussels in salt water or wine in a deep, covered kettle over high heat, agitating, for 6-8 minutes, or until shells have opened.

Sauté garlic and shallots until transparent. Serve with mussels.
Serves 3-6.

Steamed Fillets and Greens

4 fillets (1½-2 lbs.) cod, haddock or pollock
1-3 lbs. turnip, beet, dandelion, mustard, kale or other greens
2 cups water
1 cup dry white wine
1 tablespoon dry mustard
1 teaspoon salt

Wash and towel dry greens and place in large kettle. Add water, wine, mustard and salt. Cover, bring to a boil and simmer for 10 minutes.

Rinse and dry fillets. Place fillets on top of greens, cover tightly and simmer 15-20 minutes or until fish is cooked. Serve fillets, unwrapped on bed of greens with lemon butter or hollandaise sauce.
Serves 4.

Fish Chowder

12 medium potatoes, peeled & diced
3 lbs. haddock, cut in 1-2-inch pieces
2 medium onions
6 slices bacon, coarsely chopped, or cubed salt pork
    or 3 tablespoons vegetable oil
4 tablespoons flour
4 tablespoons butter
2 cups milk
2 teaspoons salt
¼ teaspoon white pepper
½ teaspoon paprika
1 cup cream

    Boil potatoes in lightly salted water for 10 minutes, or until partially cooked, but firm. Drain.
    Fry bacon or salt pork — or heat vegetable oil — over medium heat in bottom of a large heavy saucepan or kettle. Add onions and cook until translucent. Add flour and combine to make a paste.
    Reduce heat. Add milk, cream, butter, potatoes, haddock, salt, pepper and paprika. Simmer, but do not allow to boil, for ½ hour.
    Serves 6.

Fisherman's Stew

1½ lbs. haddock, cod or halibut
1 lb. scrubbed and bearded mussels
4 cups water
1 cup white wine
1 19-oz. can tomatoes
1 6-oz. can tomato paste
1 medium onion, chopped
4 leeks, coarsely chopped
2 cloves garlic

¹/₂ cup chopped celery leaves
2 bay leaves
a pinch of saffron
2 teaspoons salt
¹/₄ teaspoon pepper

Melt butter in bottom of large kettle. Sauté onion, leeks, garlic and celery leaves until wilted. Stir in flour. Add water, tomatoes, wine, tomato paste, bay leaves, saffron, salt and pepper. Cut fillets into 1-inch cubes. Add to pot with scallops. Reduce heat and simmer 10 minutes. Add mussels, in shell, and simmer 5 minutes or until mussels open.
Serves 4-6.

Lobster Bisque

3 tablespoons butter
2 shallots, finely chopped
¹/₄ cup celery, finely chopped
3 tablespoons flour
2 cups milk
1 cup cream
8 ounces cooked lobster, diced
cayenne
¹/₂ teaspoon salt
(1 tablespoon canned lobster paste)
(dash of dry sherry)

Melt butter in saucepan. Add celery and shallots and cook over medium heat until shallots are translucent. Stir in flour. Add cream, milk and cayenne. Cook over low heat until slightly thickened and smooth. Add lobster and continue cooking only until lobster is heated. Remove 1 cup of mixture, including lobster, and place in blender and blend until smooth. Combine with remaining bisque and serve garnished with fresh parsley.
Serves 4.

Baking

Tuna Loaf

2 eggs
¼ cup milk
1 tablespoon soft butter
½ teaspoon salt
¼ teaspoon paprika
1 teaspoon lemon juice
2 cups cooked, flaked tuna (or 2-7½ oz. cans)
1 cup fine bread crumbs
2 tablespoons chopped parsley
½ teaspoon minced fresh tarragon

If you can get fresh tuna, use it.

Preheat oven to 400° F. Beat eggs, milk, butter, salt, paprika and lemon juice. Add tuna, bread crumbs, parsley and tarragon. Press into greased loaf pan and bake 30-35 minutes.

May be served hot or cold.

Haddock Baked in Milk

1½ lbs. haddock fillets
½ cup flour
1 teaspoon salt
⅛ teaspoon white pepper
3 tablespoons butter
milk sufficient to almost cover fillets

Preheat oven to 325° F. Rinse and pat dry fillets. Combine flour, salt and white pepper and dredge fillets. Discard flour mixture. Place in bottom of buttered casserole. Add milk and dot with butter. Bake, covered for 30 minutes.
Serves 4.

Any fresh fillets with a mild flavour, such as cod, pollock, halibut or turbot may be substituted.

Stuffed Halibut

A 3-4 lb. whole small halibut
½ cup butter
2 cups bread crumbs
1 cup chopped onion
1 cup celery, chopped
½ cup fresh parsley, chopped
1 teaspoon salt
¼ teaspoon pepper
½ teaspoon summer savory

Prepare stuffing: melt butter over medium heat. Add onions, celery, pepper and savory and sauté until onions are translucent. Stir in bread crumbs.

Preheat oven to 350° F. Rinse and wipe halibut and stuff cavity. Place in centre of piece of aluminum foil placed on a baking sheet and dot with additional butter. Draw ends of foil over stuffed fish and fold edges together to seal. Bake for 45 minutes. Peel back foil and bake for 15 minutes more.
Serves 6-8.

Scallops Baked in Hollandaise

1 lb. scallops
1 cup hollandaise (packaged or see below)
3 medium potatoes
paprika

Peel and quarter potatoes and boil in lightly salted water until soft. Drain, mash, add 2 tablespoons hollandaise and whip.
Preheat oven to 325° F.
Rinse scallops under cool water and pat dry.
Fill small baking dish with scallops and pour on remaining hollandaise. Pipe whipped potatoes through pastry bag around edge of baking dish. Sprinkle with paprika and bake for 25-30 minutes until potato is golden and scallops are cooked.
Serves 2-4.

Blender Hollandaise:
½ cup butter
3 egg yolks
2 tablespoons lemon juice
¼ teaspoon salt
cayenne or hot sauce

Heat butter until bubbly, but not brown. Place egg yolks, lemon juice, salt and pinch of cayenne or dash of hot sauce in blender and blend on high. Open cover and pour in melted butter in steady stream. Blend for 5-10 seconds after butter is added. Use immediately or keep warm.
Makes one cup.

Stuffed Trout

2 cleaned, whole trout, ¾ lb. each
½ cup bread crumbs
2 shallots (or 1 small onion)

¼ cup diced celery
1 teaspoon lemon juice
2 tablespoons oil
2 teaspoons butter

Rinse and dry trout. Sprinkle cavity with salt, pepper and lemon juice.

Sauté shallots and celery in oil and butter until onions are translucent, and combine with bread crumbs. Add salt, pepper, parsley and lemon juice. Stuff trout. Place trout on broiling pan or shallow baking dish and dot with additional butter. Bake for 30 minutes in a 350° F oven or until skin crackles and flesh flakes. **Serves 2.**

Sole with Crab Stuffing

4 sole fillets (1-1½ lb.)
½ cup bread crumbs
3 tablespoons butter
¼ cup chopped shallots
4-oz. salad crabmeat
¼ cup cream
¼ teaspoon salt
¼ teaspoon pepper
1 tablespoon dry or 3 tablespoons fresh parsley

Prepare stuffing: Melt butter over medium heat. Sauté shallots until translucent. Add crabmeat and stir until heated throughout. Sprinkle with salt, pepper and parsley and stir in cream. Combine with bread crumbs.

Preheat oven to 350° F. Grease a low-sided baking dish or oven proof platter. Rinse and pat dry fillets and arrange in bottom of baking dish. Spoon stuffing onto each fillet and bake for 15 minutes or until stuffing is golden.

Haddock, cod, pollock fillets may be substituted for sole. Chopped celery or mushrooms may also be added to stuffing.

Scallops Wrapped in Bacon

1 lb. scallops
½ lb. bacon
small skewers

Cut bacon in half. Broil bacon until top side has begun to crisp and ends of strips curl up. Cool slightly.

Rinse and dry scallops. Wrap each with a bacon strip, uncooked side out, and skewer. Arrange under broiler and cook for 10 minutes, turning once, until bacon is cooked.

Makes 25-35.

Zucchini Boats

½ lb. shrimp
½ lb. scallops
2 small zucchini
1 onion, finely chopped
2 tablespoons butter
2 tablespoons flour
1 cup milk
4 tablespoons grated parmesan cheese
2 teaspoons paprika
½ teaspoon salt

Parboil whole zucchini for 3 minutes. Slice in half lengthwise. Scoop out seeds. Also scoop out and chop ½ cup zucchini, leaving four "boats".

Sauté chopped zucchini and onion in butter. Sprinkle with flour and stir to combine. Stir in milk, salt and paprika, and simmer, stirring until mixture thickens. Finally, mix in 2 tablespoons grated parmesan, scallops and shrimp. Fill boats and top with remaining parmesan. Broil 8 minutes or until golden brown.

Serves 4.

Oysters Parmesan

24 oysters on the half shell
⅓ cup butter
3 shallots, or 1 small onion, finely chopped
3 tablespoons chopped fresh parsley
2 tablespoons lemon juice
¼ cup grated parmesan

Preheat oven to 450° F. Melt butter over medium heat. Remove and combine with shallots and parsley. Distribute mixture over oysters. Sprinkle with lemon juice and cheese. Bake for 5 to 8 minutes, or until parmesan is golden.
Serves 4.

Haddock Loaf

1 lb. haddock fillets
¼ cup onion, chopped
½ teaspoon dill
½ cup milk
1 tablespoon butter
¼ cup chopped celery
1 cup fresh coarse bread crumbs
½ teaspoon dried tarragon
2 eggs, separated
dash of hot sauce

Preheat oven to 375° F. In a saucepan, cover fillets with lightly salted water. Bring to a boil, reduce heat, cover and cook until fish flakes. Sauté onion and celery in butter for three minutes. In a bowl, mix flaked fish, celery, onions, crumbs, tarragon, dill and salt. Beat yolks and add milk and hot sauce. Add to fish mixture. Beat egg whites until stiff but not dry and fold into mixture. Spread evenly in a well buttered loaf pan. Set pan in hot water and bake for 40 minutes.
Serves 4.

Seafood Newburg

1 lb. haddock
½ lb. shrimp, peeled and deveined
½ lb. scallops
¼ cup butter
1 cup mushrooms, sliced
¼ cup flour
1 teaspoon dry mustard
1 teaspoon salt
pinch cayenne
2 cups milk
1 teaspoon Worcestershire sauce
1 teaspoon onion salt
2 teaspoons sherry
1 teaspoon dried parsley
½ cup sharp cheddar, grated

½ cup fresh coarse bread crumbs
1 tablespoon butter

Preheat oven to 350°F. In one-half inch of water in a saucepan, steam scallops and shrimp. Bake haddock for 6 to 8 minutes until slightly underdone.

In a double boiler melt butter and sauté mushrooms. Stir in flour, dry mustard, salt and cayenne. Add milk and stir until thickened. Add Worcestershire sauce, onion salt, sherry, parsley and cheese.

Layer seafood in a casserole dish. Pour sauce over fish. Melt remaining tablespoon of butter in a small frying pan and coat bread crumbs. Top casserole with crumbs. Bake for 30 minutes.

Serves 4-6.

Sole and Lime Pinwheels

1 lb. small sole fillets (larger fillets may be divided into smaller portions)
$^3/_4$ cup bread crumbs
6 tablespoons butter, softened
2 tablespoons chives
juice of 1 lime
grated peel from one lime

Combine butter and chives. Mix in bread crumbs, $^1/_4$ cup of the lime juice and grated peel. Spread over fillets, roll and secure with toothpicks spaced one inch apart. Slice rolls between toothpicks, sprinkle with remaining lime juice and broil six to eight inches from element for 5 minutes. Turn and broil 3 minutes longer.

Microwave recipes

Basic Microwaved Fillets

1 lb. cod, haddock or pollock fillets
1 tablespoon butter
1 teaspoon fresh lemon juice
salt and white pepper

Rinse fillets and pat dry. Grease a microwave-safe casserole. Arrange fillets with thickest edges toward the outside of the dish. Sprinkle with lemon, salt and pepper. Cover with waxed paper.

Fish cooks very quickly in a microwave. A good rule of thumb is one-fifth the time of conventional cooking methods. On average, it takes 4-5 minutes at HIGH temperature to cook 1 pound of fillets to 140°F. Like other microwaved foods, fish will continue to cook for 4-5 minutes more after microwaving. This "standing time" is crucial to successful cooking.

You should keep an eye on the fillets while they are cooking and test occasionally with a fork. Fish should be opaque and flake easily when properly cooked.

Serves 2-4

Portuguese Cod

4 cod fillets, about 1½-2 lbs.
1 cup stewed tomatoes
¼ cup tomato paste
3 tablespoons olive oil
1 medium onion, chopped
2 cloves garlic, crushed
1 tablespoon dry basil (or 3 tablespoons chopped fresh)
1 teaspoon dry oregano (or 1 tablespoon chopped fresh)
dash of hot sauce
(dash of red wine)

Heat oil in bottom of saucepan over medium heat. Add onions, garlic, basil and oregano and sauté until onions are translucent. Next add tomatoes, tomato paste, salt, hot sauce and red wine. Cook until sauce thickens, 30-45 minutes.

Rinse fillets and pat dry. Arrange in microwave-proof baking dish. Spoon sauce over top. Cover and bake at HIGH for 8-10 minutes. Let stand 5 minutes.

Serves 4.

Stuffed Fillets

1 lb. haddock or other fillets
1 cup fine bread crumbs
1 medium chopped onion
¼ cup finely chopped celery
2 tablespoons minced parsley
1 teaspoon lemon juice
1 teaspoon celery salt

Rinse and pat fillets dry. Put butter and onion in 4 cup glass measuring cup or bowl and cook on HIGH for 2 minutes. Add remaining ingredients. Butter a microwave-safe casserole dish and arrange half the fillets in it. Spoon on stuffing and top with remaining fillets. Dot with butter and cover with waxed paper. Bake on HIGH for 5-6 minutes or until fillets are flaky.

Serves 4.

Florentine Sole

1 lb. sole fillets
1 lb. fresh or 10-oz. frozen spinach
½ cup sliced mushrooms
1 small chopped onion
½ cup grated mozzarella
1 cup milk
2 tablespoons flour
½ teaspoon salt
dash of Worcestershire sauce
dash of hot sauce
a grating of nutmeg

Rinse spinach and place in covered microwave-safe casserole. Cook on HIGH for 5 minutes.

Sauté onion in medium skillet until translucent. Stir in flour to make a paste. Add milk and stir until sauce begins to thicken. Season with salt, Worcestershire, hot sauce and nutmeg. Add mushrooms and cheese and pour over spinach, reserving ¼ - ½ cup. Arrange fillets over spinach and top with remaining sauce. Cover with waxed paper and cook on HIGH for 6 minutes. Allow to stand 5 minutes before serving.
Serves 4.

This is also a tasty way to serve cod, haddock, pollock and other fillets.

Barbecueing

Barbecued Mackerel

1½ - 2 lb. cleaned, whole mackerel
1 tablespoon vegetable oil
1 teaspoon lemon juice
½ teaspoon Worcestershire sauce
¼ teaspoon dry marjoram
½ teaspoon salt
¼ teaspoon black pepper

Rinse and wipe mackerel. Puncture skin in several places with a sharp fork. Brush fish with remaining ingredients inside cavity and out.

Place fish on lightly oiled grill over moderate coals (or medium setting of gas barbecue). Barbecue 10 minutes per side, or until skin separates from the flesh and the meat pulls away from the bone when gently pried with a fork.

Serves 4.

Barbecued Whole Salmon

3-5 lb. whole, dressed salmon
1½ cups cooked rice
1 medium onion, chopped
½ cup sliced mushrooms
½ cup diced celery
½ cup dry white wine
¼ cup melted butter
1 tablespoon lemon juice
½ teaspoon dried or 1 teaspoon fresh tarragon
¼ teaspoon ground tumeric
1 teaspoon salt
¼ teaspoon cayenne pepper
additional melted butter for basting

Wipe cleaned whole salmon with a damp cloth, inside and out. Place on a double layer of foil, large enough to wrap and seal fish.

Melt butter in skillet and sauté onions and celery until onions begin to soften. Add mushrooms and cook for one minute. Combine with remaining ingredients and stuff the salmon.

Wrap salmon in foil, sealing the edges. Barbecue over moderately low heat for approximately one hour, turning every 10 minutes. Open foil and baste with melted butter several times during cooking.
Serves 6-8.

This is also an excellent way to cook a large trout.

Barbecued Whole Halibut

2-4 lb. small whole dressed halibut
4 leeks, sliced
½ cup diced celery

1 cup bread crumbs
¼ cup melted butter
1 tablespoon lemon juice
½ teaspoon salt
¼ teaspoon thyme
⅛ teaspoon black pepper

Wipe halibut inside and out with a damp cloth.

Sauté leeks and celery in melted butter. Combine with bread crumbs, lemon juice, salt, pepper and thyme. Stuff halibut, brush with butter and wrap in a double layer of foil. Barbecue over moderate coals for 30-40 minutes, or until flesh flakes and skin pulls away easily.

Serves 6.

*You may want to try the above with other whole fish such as haddock, cod or pollock. Because the flesh is less dense with these than is the case with halibut, you should handle these other fish **very gently**.*

Grilled Swordfish Steaks

4 swordfish steaks, ¾ inch thick
¼ cup melted butter
2 tablespoons lemon juice
1 clove garlic, crushed
dash of hot sauce

Brush swordfish with other ingredients and grill over moderately hot coals for 8 to 10 minutes turning and basting as needed.

Serves 4.

This method also works well with other meaty fish steaks such as shark, tuna or shad.

Fish Kabobs

1 lb. scallops
1 lb. large shrimp (16-24 per pound)
½ lb. bacon
12-16 pearl onions
12-16 cherry tomatoes
2 green peppers
½ cup soy sauce
2 tablespoons vegetable oil
1 medium onion, chopped
1 clove garlic, crushed
1 teaspoon ground ginger
1 teaspoon dry mustard

Combine soy sauce, oil, chopped onion, garlic, ginger and mustard to make marinade.

Wrap each scallop in ½ slice of bacon, and skewer with other ingredients, alternating between shellfish and vegetables. Marinate 4 to 6 hours, refrigerated.

Barbecue over moderately high coals, turning and brushing with marinade 3-5 minutes or until bacon is crisp and shrimp are cooked.

Serves 6-8.

While the above is our favorite recipe for fish kabobs, experiment with other small chunks of seafood and vegetables. Some even like a little red meat interspersed with the other ingredients on the skewer.

Deep Frying

Fish n' Chips

1½-2 lbs. haddock fillets
4 medium potatoes
1 cup milk
2 eggs
1 cup flour
1 teaspoon salt
2 teaspoons baking powder
additional flour for dusting fish

Preheat deep fryer to 375°F.

Rinse and wipe fish and cut into 3-4 inch chunks. Dust with flour.

In a bowl, beat eggs and milk. Sift together flour, salt and baking powder and add to liquid. Dip fish pieces in batter, coating thoroughly. Fry 10-12 minutes or until golden and crispy. Drain on absorbent paper.

For chips, scrub potatoes and remove eyes and blemishes. Cut into ¼-inch strips. Towel dry. Fry 8-10 minutes, or until crispy. Allow to drain briefly in fryer basket or a wire strainer and then on absorbent paper.

Serve with ketchup and white vinegar.
Serves 4.

For an unusual treat, substitute salmon for haddock.

Digby Scallops with Tartar Sauce

1-1½ lbs. scallops
2 cups flour
2 teaspoons salt
2 cups milk
½ cup mayonnaise
2 tablespoons sweet pickle relish
1 teaspoon lemon juice

Preheat deep fryer to 375°F.

Rinse and dry scallops. In a medium-sized mixing bowl, combine flour and salt. Pour milk into a second bowl. Coat scallops in flour mixture, dip in milk and coat once more in flour. Deep fry 5-8 minutes, or until golden and crisp. Drain on absorbent paper.

For tartar sauce, combine mayonnaise, relish and lemon juice. Serve with scallops.

Serves 4.

Seafood Tempura

½ lb. salmon, cut in 1-2 inch pieces
½ lb. shrimp
1 cup shelled clams
1 bunch green onions
3 stalks celery
1 large green pepper
1½ cups flour
1½ cups water
2 egg yolks
1 teaspoon salt

Preheat deep fryer to 375°F. Rinse and dry salmon. Shell and remove back vein from shrimp. Cut celery into ¼-inch sticks, 4 inches long. Cut 2 slits, 1-inch long, in one end of stick. Cut green onions into 4-inch pieces, and make one slit, 1-inch long in end of stalk. Soak in iced water for 1 hour, or until ends curl. Slice pepper into $1/4$-inch strips. Sift flour and salt together. Make a well in center, add water and egg yolks and beat until glossy. Coat seafood and vegetables in tempura and fry until crisp.

Serves 4-6.

Cold and/or Quick

Shrimp Cocktail

1 lb. cooked cocktail shrimp
¼ cup tomato sauce
1 teaspoon red wine vinegar
2 teaspoons sugar
2 tablespoons grated horseradish
4-6 drops hot sauce
¼ teaspoon salt
small head of lettuce
fresh parsley and lemon wedges for garnish.

Wash, shell - leaving tails intact, and remove the dark coloured vein that runs along the back of each shrimp by gently slitting with a sharp paring knife and pulling gently or carefully scraping with the tip of the blade. Chill thoroughly.

Blend tomato paste, vinegar, sugar, horseradish, hot sauce and salt. Line 4 deep, small bowls or stemmed dessert glasses with the lettuce. Divide sauce between bowls. Arrange chilled shrimp around outside edge of bowls, tails out. Garnish with parsley and lemon.
Serves 4.

Smoked Mackerel Paté

½ lb. smoked mackerel
2 tablespoon lemon juice
8 oz. soft cream cheese
½ cup finely diced green pepper
1 tablespoon butter
2 tablespoons minced onion
½ teaspoon fennel seed
¼ teaspoon black pepper

In a food processor blend skinned, boned mackerel, lemon juice, cream cheese, butter and spices. Remove from food processor. Mix in green pepper. Press into a bowl and refrigerate, covered, for at least 3 hours.

Salmon Loaf

1 lb. cooked, flaked salmon or 2 cans (7-oz. each)
2 eggs, beaten
½ cup milk
2 tablespoons minced onion
1 tablespoon lemon juice
½ teaspoon dried tarragon
½ teaspoon salt
¼ teaspoon pepper
2 cups fine bread crumbs

Preheat oven to 350°F. Combine ingredients and press into greased loaf pan. Bake 50-60 minutes or until loaf is firm, top is golden and its sides have separated from the pan. Serve hot or cold with a dollop of mayonnaise.
Serves 4-6.

Seafood Sub

1 loaf French bread
1 small head lettuce
2 tomatoes
½ cup alfalfa sprouts
8-oz. salad crab
4-oz. smoked salmon

¼ cup mayonnaise
2 tablespoons dijon mustard

butter
salt
pepper

Slice French bread lengthwise, butter and assemble ingredients in layers, finishing with top crust. Slice diagonally in four pieces.
Serves 4.

Leftover Melts

8-oz. cooked haddock, cod, sole or other leftover fish, flaked
4 English muffins
4 tablespoons mayonnaise
1 tablespoon prepared mustard
2 tablespoons finely diced onion
16 cooked asparagus spears
½ cup grated cheddar

Split English muffins. Combine mayonnaise and mustard and spread on muffin halves. Divide asparagus between muffins and distribute flaked fish. Top with cheddar and onions. Broil 3-5 minutes until cheese melts and muffins are heated.
Serves 4.

Hot Crab Dip

Mix and heat:
8-oz. cream cheese
6 tablespoons mayonnaise
1 medium onion, grated
½ teaspoon prepared mustard
2 tablespoons chili sauce
1 tablespoon parsley

Fold in 1 can(6½-oz) crabmeat. Top with 2 tablespoons melted butter and ½ cup bread crumbs. Bake at 375°F for 25 minutes. Serve warm with crackers.

Tuna Salad

8-oz. cooked flaked tuna
1 small onion, chopped
2 cups cooked macaroni
1 cup celery
½ cup diced green pepper
¼ cup chopped fresh parsley
sprinkle of black pepper
½ cup mayonnaise

Combine ingredients and chill well before serving. **Serves 4.**

Smoked, Salted, Pickled and Dried

Solomon Suzie

³/₄-1 lb. turbot
³/₄-1 lb. halibut
1½ cups white wine vinegar
½ cup water
2 medium onions, thinly sliced
1 carrot thinly sliced
1 stalk celery, cut in thin strips
¼ cup pickling spices, tied in cheesecloth
2 tablespoons white vinegar
¼ cup vegetable oil

Rinse and wipe fillets, and cut into 2-3 inch pieces. Lightly salt, place in covered casserole and microwave or bake in moderate oven until slightly undercooked. Arrange in bottom of large crockery or glass bowl.

Combine remaining ingredients, except oil, in kettle, bring to a boil and simmer for 20 minutes. Pour hot pickle over fish. Coat with a layer of oil, cover and refrigerate for 1 week, replenishing oil as necessary.

Fish Cakes

5-oz. dried salt pollock or cod
6 medium potatoes
1 medium onion, chopped
1 tablespoon butter
¼ teaspoon pepper
1 egg
1 teaspoon water
flour for dredging

Soak the salt fish in water overnight.

Peel, boil and drain potatoes. Add onion and salt fish to pot. Mash until well combined. Make into hamburger-sized patties. Dredge with flour and place between layers of waxed paper in refrigerator until thoroughly chilled. Beat egg and water. Dip cakes in egg mixture and dredge with flour. Melt butter in large skillet over moderate heat. Cook, turning once, until golden and crispy.

Makes 12 fish cakes.

Creamed Smoked Cod

1-1½ lbs. smoked cod
2 tablespoons butter
1 large onion, thinly sliced
1 cup water
1 hard boiled egg, coarsely chopped
½ cup milk
1 heaping tablespoon flour

Bring water to boil. Add cod, butter and onion and simmer 4 minutes. In a small jar or covered container, shake together milk and flour. Pour into pan with cod, simmer and stir until broth thickens. Add chopped egg. Serve on toast or puffed pastry.

Serves 4.

Baked Finnan Haddie

1 split finnan haddie, skin and bones removed (or 1 lb. smoked haddock fillets)
4 tablespoons butter
2 tablespoons flour
1 cup milk
2 egg yolks
½ cup bread crumbs
2 tablespoons fresh, chopped chives
½ teaspoon salt
1 cup cooked rice

Preheat oven to 350°F. Melt 2 tablespoons butter and stir in flour and salt. Gradually add milk and stir until mixture thickens. Remove from heat. Beat egg yolks. Gradually add two tablespoons sauce to egg, stirring to combine. Add to sauce. Stir in fish. Arrange rice in bottom of greased casserole dish. Pour finnan haddie mixture over rice. Melt remaining butter and combine with bread crumbs and chives. Distribute over fish and bake 30 minutes, or until crust is golden.
Serves 4 - 6.

Smoked Salmon & Snow Pea Fettuccine

½ lb. fresh fettuccine (or 1½ cups dry packaged)
1 lb. snow peas
4-oz. sour cream
8-oz. smoked salmon, finely sliced

Combine cream cheese and sour cream and set aside. Cook fettuccine in 2 quarts water. Drain. Stir cream and cheese mixture, snow peas and smoked salmon into pasta. Serve immediately. The heat from the pasta is sufficient to heat the added ingredients.
Serves 4.

Smoked Salmon Quiche

Baked 9-inch pie shell
8-oz. smoked salmon
2-3 leeks, washed and sliced
1 tablespoon butter
1 cup grated Swiss cheese
4 eggs
1 cup milk or light cream
½ teaspoon salt
¼ teaspoon pepper
pinch of nutmeg

Preheat oven to 350°F.

Sauté leeks in butter until tender. Mix leeks and smoked salmon and place in bottom of pie shell. Sprinkle with cheese. Beat together eggs, milk, salt, pepper and nutmeg. Pour into pie shell and bake for 30 minutes or until firm and golden.

Serves 6.

Rolled Mops

1 lb. filleted salt herring
3 cups white vinegar
¼ cup sugar
1 medium onion, thinly sliced
3 tablespoons pickling spice
dill pickles

Combine vinegar, sugar, onion and spices and bring to a boil. Reduce heat and simmer 15-20 minutes until onions are soft. Slice pickles, lengthwise, into ¼-inch strips. Wrap each piece in a herring fillet and secure with a toothpick. Place in a casserole. Pour pickling mixture over rolls. Cover and refrigerate for a minimum of three days.

Unusual fish dishes

Steak with Lobster Sauce

4 one-inch thick tenderloin or eye-of-round steaks
1 tablespoon vegetable oil
1 tablespoon butter
6-8 oz. lobster meat
½ cup half and half or cereal cream
½ teaspoon Worcestershire sauce
sprinkling of fresh tarragon
freshly ground pepper
fresh parsley for garnish

Heat cast iron or heavy skillet. Add oil and cook steaks preferred amount. Set aside on warm platter. Add butter and pepper to drippings and stir in lobster. Increase heat to medium-high, stir in cream, Worcestershire, tarragon and cook rapidly, stirring and scraping pan until sauce thickens. Serve over steak, garnished with parsley.
Serves 4.

Seafood Pizza

½ lb. salmon fillet, cut in 1-inch chunks
½ lb. scallops, cut in quarters
½ lb. salad shrimp
½ lb. bacon, coarsely chopped and partially cooked
1½ cups grated mozzarella

Sauce:

1 cup tomato sauce
2 tablespoons vegetable oil
1 clove garlic, crushed
1 small onion, chopped
1 teaspoon salt
1 teaspoon dried basil
1 teaspoon dried oregano
½ teaspoon fennel seed
½ teaspoon horseradish

Dough:

½ cup lukewarm water
1 tablespoon sugar
½ package active dry yeast
2 teaspoons vegetable oil
1½ cups flour
½ teaspoon salt

Make dough: Dissolve sugar and yeast in water and allow to proof 10 minutes. Add oil. Sift in flour and salt, mixing to combine several times during process. Knead on floured board for 5 minutes. Set aside in greased, covered bowl to rise while making the sauce.

In a medium skillet over moderate heat, sauté garlic and onion until transparent. Add remaining spices, tomato sauce and horseradish and simmer 15-20 minutes. Allow to cool.

Preheat oven to 400°F. Roll or toss dough to fit one greased pizza pan. Cover with sauce. Top with salmon, scallops, shrimp and bacon and cover with grated cheese. Bake 20 minutes or until cheese is golden and crusty.

Serves 6.

Caribbean Fish Chowder

2 lbs. monk fish, in 1-2 inch cubes
½ lb. scallops, quartered
¼ lb. bacon
2 medium onions, chopped
1 clove garlic, crushed
1 green pepper, diced
2 stalks celery, chopped
1 lb. fresh, or 1 can stewed tomatoes, mashed
2 cups water
1 bay leaf
¼ teaspoon cloves
½ teaspoon thyme
1 tablespoon Worcestershire sauce
4 medium potatoes, diced
2 carrots, sliced
5-10 drops hot sauce (or to taste)
salt to taste
1-2 oz. dark rum (or to taste)
1 tablespoon dry sherry (or to taste)

Sauté bacon, onions and garlic in bottom of large kettle. Add green pepper and celery and stir until softened. Stir in remaining ingredients, except seafood and liquor, bring to a boil, reduce heat and simmer at least 1 hour. Fifteen minutes before serving, add fish, scallops, rum and sherry.
Serves 6-8.

Index